Harmony

NEW AND SELECTED POEMS

For Chris Marchese —
With my very best
wishes!

Bill Rewak, S.J.

William J. Rewak

ISBN: 1539052559
ISBN 13: 9781539052555
Library of Congress Control Number: 2016916143
CreateSpace Independent Publishing Platform
North Charleston, South Carolina

For my brother Jesuits

How sweet the moonlight sleeps upon this bank!
Here will we sit, and let the sounds of music
Creep in our ears; soft stillness and the night
Become the touches of sweet harmony.

William Shakespeare
The Merchant of Venice,
act 5, sc. 1

Table of Contents

HARMONY

New Poems

The Gulls

Open up to a page
any page
and look for the words
that today you can juggle
(tomorrow is another page)
and when they're all in the air
and your breath is still
you'll discover another
message, not envisioned,
but it's there
for only a flickering
that rare opening
when you see the cliffs
and the sea
the gulls stretching in the wind
when what you know
is transformed
and the sheer silken notion
is born
that words can grow beyond
themselves
they can catch the wings
of the gulls
and soar.

Effulgence

I want you to look at this,
  this petal, deep blue,

springing from the earth in all
  its glory and expecting you to look;

it's primed itself, washed and preened
  so you'll notice; such petals

have abandoned humility for the favor
  we bestow on them, and I wonder

if they know the hours are few,
  if they understand how their edges will crinkle

and the earth will welcome them back –
  but that's no matter because their effulgence

overrides mortality.

Peanut

I've a pile of dry roasted
peanuts next to me as I type
so I can take advantage of a calorie
or two as I plow through
my right brain to uncover
the nuggets buried there,
my own peanuts that set
my mind ablaze: they are still,
unyielding, devoid of color
but, like all seeds and nuts,
with an inner strength that will,
with appropriate TLC, blossom
into the wild gardens I see
outside my window and fill
the thirsty, waiting world
with the sharp scent of life
or they'll grow into the comedies
that spin off my fingers
and settle lightly on our days
or erupt onto canvases that dazzle
our eyes with colors of all
the rainbows, or I can be a sly
graffiti artist and splash
every wall with messages
from deep in the earth and thus
be a prophet unafraid who sees
the heart and points the way.

Or – I can remain a nerd
with nothing more to do
than philosophize on the life force
of a peanut.

Exiting

From London to Edinburgh on a sleek
overnight train I slept restlessly

dreaming of myself on a train with a boisterous
crowd rolling through sheep-encrusted

fields of green with sight interrupted
too often by hedgerows, but it was the crowd

I watched as sightlines changed among them,
as hands reached and then veered off

in another direction; words rose
to the ceiling and finding no purchase

fell to the floor where they got stomped on;
coats eventually were discarded and everyone

seemed ready for the next installment
when unaccountably the train stopped and most,

with a flustered indecision, exited; I was left
with four or five subdued passengers

who sat quietly, tried to salvage
some of the words scattered on the floor

and kept their eyes carefully fixed
on the next exit while slipping on their coats.

Fields turned amber and blue
as heather rushed by, and I slept more soundly.

Games

To take a word,
"inconsequentiality," for example,
and play with it as a child
toys with a new balloon
fit it to Heidegger, Julius Caesar's Rome,

the redundant images on a movie screen
watch it jump about
in metrical determination
and musical distance –
that is the joy and surprise of a poem.

Block

for Jim Torrens, S.J.

Sometimes I'm just empty
no food down there in the belly
and the fancy so unfanciful
all I see is a white sheet:

let's follow that up,
let's draw closer,
look hard,
gotta be something.

Grab a corner, pull,
and hope I'm a magician
with bunnies and mirrors and handcuffs
ready to delight any crowd,

pick up a saw maybe and start sawing
and look to see if she is still whole,
wield a wand and watch a white tiger
bound onto the page;

just so there's life,
nerves crackling,
desire,
a pulse that races to the finish line.

The First Day

In that moment
when You stepped onto our earth
was sound something new:
the bleating of sheep,
the soft swish of wind, a voice
that blanketed You with whispers
of joy;
did You see, for the first time, the sparkles
and colors of the night?

Did her face fill Your eyes?
When You felt the strength
that kept Your body warm,
did You turn in wonder?

Were You pleased
with the freshness of a word,
how shadows moved,
the sure ground they all stood on
(the dense texture of wood)?

Did You smell the straw
and could you taste the evening?

Did You see a toy in a winging dove?

Was it all a great surprise?

You stretched Your hand to touch
And You found it good.

The Parasol

She was determined that at her acceptable end
she'd gracefully wave goodbye and board
the late train she knew would be waiting for her
because she was a First Class passenger, with class,
and trains knew their business, so here,
now, she carefully packs cosmetics,
see-through lingerie and a rainbowed parasol
because she's always prepared, but most especially
she places inside a knock-off Gucci bag
her leather address book because contrary
to what she's been told, she's certain she'll be phoning
her friends and showing up at their front door
for continued conversations about how they slighted her:
not to distress them with post-prandial
apparitions – she has no wish to elicit gastric
interruptions – but to calmly state her probity
which she wore with resolve as warriors their spears.
Oh, she knew the difference between a hyacinth
and a morning glory as she could tell the difference
between a smile and a smirk, and catching a wink
in a mirror once she placed her guest in a lower
seat, but she seldom exacted revenge,
it marred her complexion and made her wonder
about morality – on which she often pondered and just
as often concluded she needn't bother wondering.
The time is here, she clicks her suitcase shut,
springs open her rainbowed parasol

and lets it lie fetchingly on her left
shoulder, then reaches for the hand to guide her,
while listening for the whistle - so far
out on the edge; why so far away?

The Beauty Parlor

"The rage for beauty is toxic"
(3rd century philosopher from Antarctica)

Just imagine you're sitting in a unisex parlor
enjoying a haircut and discussing tax increases
when a walrus shuffles in demanding a shave;
the hair stylist tells him to sit and wait,
so the walrus slumps against a chair, pouting.

(He recalls he once asked God if he could be
a gazelle so he could spring and pose in elegance,
but nothing happened so he figured what he is
is all there is. He pondered often the discrepancies
in nature and how beauty is distributed so unevenly;
he arrived at no conclusion other than that God
probably doesn't know the difference. Nevertheless,
this did not prevent him from the occasional shave
and shampoo, a stringent exercise routine, an annual
skin-tightening regime, and a good tusk-polishing.)

Just imagine his bulk getting restless: best to bow
to his immensity and concede your place to someone
so determined to subvert the order of things.

Preparation

Whether you know it or not
you're preparing: every time

you open a can of beans
or walk a lily-lined path

kiss your child or write
your latest essay that will set

ears blazing, every
time you sit and watch

an icicle slowly slough off
its crinkled shape: each

is filled with the right ingredients;
the soufflé that results is a wild

tangy taste of the glorious
time to come.

A Chocolate

for Pat Schott

I'll tell you about my grandmother:
she was no slipshod Nellie, her back

was always straight and when she played
poker her smile was hidden

behind a gaze that dared anyone
to best her; she knew nothing

about wars and the useless meanderings
of the current politicos because her life's

choices were deeper than time:
time floated above her in constant

and irresponsible change; but her laughter
healed the rifts and losses.

She met a child once
who saluted her in a park and asked

if she knew where God was; she patted
his cheek and gave him a chocolate:

that seemed to solve his problem –
she was good at solving problems.

But she knew the edge of the cliff
and was not afraid to walk it:

for though the sun was always in her voice
there was a violet evening in her eyes.

Walking

I like walking
where trees shield
my careful thoughts:
it gives me a review
of the day, an auditor
settling the accounts,

a black line
here where love
is added to the plus,
a red line
there where sins
upend the balance.

But each step
is a new digit
to be argued over
because we cannot
be sure what the final
tally will be;

so I keep walking
and counting the steps
with a hard-won
faith that each
step makes
a difference.

A Wren

A wren it is
just a bird,
but trying to be
more than it is;
it has soft wings
and trills
in the morning
reaching for an aria
to rival Mimì;
one of the least,
it wants the seat
at the head
of the table;
it sees a great
wingspan in the air
and flies to greet it
as a comrade
but did not know
about hawks.

The Halls of Congress

Put your bunny hat
away and grow up;
put on a deerstalker
        or top hat;
be Holmes or Astaire
show us some wit
        and lilt,
play the violin
and dance, confound
us, show us life.
It's too late
to rattle around
        in a playpen,
this hopping-to-nowhere.

"... and to Dust..."

She slipped slowly
  all the threads breaking,
her hands at rest now,
white on white.

No matter the multitudinous
times it happens,
it never bores
  nor does it age
a fearsome thing we meet each time with surprise;

the smell of it clutches our throat:
no gold chariot
  to ride into the blue

only a harsh raven
caught in the bottom of a well.

The Book

She sat by her favorite window
holding a book on her lap
not attending to its words
and its warnings, just rubbing
her thumb along its leather cover
and wondering how the day would end.

The green drapes on either
side of the window reflected
both the sedate lawn outside
and the green car that had pulled up
in front of her house. She waited
all day for its doors to open.

She turned the book over
in her hands, riffled the pages,
but nothing begged for notice
and she thought back to her lemonade
stand because that was much cheaper
than these words, and tasted better.

With some effort she stood,
threw the silent book
at the window and watched the glass
snap and fall at her feet
while the green drapes stirred
in the respectful evening breeze.

Certitude

THEY OFFERED IT TO ME free: I walked in through the blue door and was greeted by a red-lipped teenager who took my name and asked me why I was born. I must have mistaken her words, so mellifluous they seemed, but she asked again and I said it was God's decision but what I really want is a new iPhone; she took me by the arm and in the shadows of a corner protected by samples of iPhones, earphones, iPads and other wonders that have redrawn the contours of our lives she asked if I was serious about God; well, I said, of course, and she said she had once rolled in waves off a beach in Maui and was caught in a maelstrom of bubbles and her life had since never been bubble-free, so she thought maybe God was a harsh creator of bubbles and did not care how they interrupted a daily swim; well, I was flabbergasted and hesitantly said perhaps bubbles are not the troubles you think they are but little pearls to breeze your skin lightly and show you the colors that burst through the mist each morning, and she looked at me and brushed a speck of dirt off her sleeve, then sighed and said that if we knew how the bubbles were born we could discern their purpose, and that is the point, she said; well, I was nonplussed, so I hitched up my pants and was about to give her a dose of homiletic certitude when she asked, "How may I help you today?"

Manna

for Geoff and Joyce Long

You put ham
and cheese together
and make a sandwich,

and this is a simple
thing to do, the kitchen
will applaud: no planets

will stop in their orbit
to marvel at your culinary
expertise, but it's like mixing

cement, weaving
a glorious eye-popping
carpet, sewing together

a winsome prayer
that tastes and smells
as if it erupted from a lonely

heart – all these are confections
we take for granted
but are meant to be savored

because they build the house
we live in, they are the manna
that has fallen like rain.

West Egg

The dark stars
fall freely
during this wanton summer
memorializing my dreams
of pink shawls
and green clicking oars
that splash and wing
to the tune
of the latest
the very latest
ragtime
melodies.

Hummingbird

A hummingbird
in the heart
You are,
magical and light,
settling softly,
but quick to note
the ripples,
to tend them;
in a movement
so swift
You can fly
and leave us
waiting
on the edge
of forgetfulness,
wandering,
until Your wings,
invisible,
alight again.

Arachnoid Tempo

(". . . there will be more terrorist attacks.
More innocent lives will be lost."
New York Times, July 16, 2016)

On nights when a gold moon
rules, the elves click
their heels to the tune
of spider music.
               You didn't know
spiders make music?
Daddy-long-legs recall
Debussy: controlled, ticklish,
with silver filaments of melody.
Black widows spin out
Berlioz with a vengeance; tarantulas
hum Tchaikovsky (it is rumored
they have created a minor "Swan Lake"
that has set the spider world
on its ear).
          Lately, the strains
are hard to catch: wild smoke
from over the hills has forced
the elves inside deep caves
and the moon now is seldom golden.

My Last Affair

If you come over here next to the staircase
I'll show you the door I haven't opened for years
because what happened down there I've tried
to forget, even though she'd not want me to,
but she never was able to understand the delicacy
of mingling fact and memory, of how each morning
we step carefully into the day, carrying the burden
of all our past hours and try to align them
in a logical sequence so they can be viewed with certitude;
she liked to pick them all up and juggle them
as if what we had been doing was only a game
and not the serious scenario I had laid out for us,
the black-and-white plan we had agreed on
that summer when she wore white silk
in a loving breeze and the bougainvillea vine
outside our window threw little diamond
shadows on the wall, when even the frenzied
valets tried to brush against her arm –
and she enjoyed the attention much as a duchess would -
but then her laugh caught in my throat and I decided
we would continue, that the road held no sharp
curves, even though the curve of her shoulder
gave me pause, for it was calculated to distract,
and I cannot be distracted from a defined itinerary.
Here, let me go first, the light is dim
and your official clothes might rub the dust

that's collected here; I would not want to be charged also with a cleaning bill. There, now you can see it: my own little rag and bone shop.

Sentence

I got into the car
then decided it was looking
the wrong way

so I decided to walk
but the leaves crackling
distracted me so I turned

back, then to the right
and passed two boys
playing catch

and wondered if the back-and-forth
ever got tiring,
sat and watched

a bit until the moon
rose over the old
cedar tree

glistening the leaves
just right –
now, there's a conclusion -

then turned left
mumbling the words
of Crazy Jane

about how all things,
finally, remain with God
then turned back

up a winding hill
that reached for an end
around a dark corner

where fireflies began
to blink like an SOS
warning and I had to stop

on the edge of the curb
look both ways
and bow my head:

my soul is a gnarled
sentence trying
to unravel itself.

Everything

in honor of Ignatius Loyola

I follow from afar
his light as it burnishes
the stones up the path
and push my way
through broken limbs
and the lush ferns
that grow to my height:
a welcoming green
by day but traitorous
in its winding by night;
though he keeps on
and with his light I see
the tricks and hollows
and keep safe.

He never trips
or stops to wonder
because he knows the way,
simple as that.
He had found it
through loving years
through seasons of ice,
through mapping the tears
of travelers and all
the ghosts he mourned;
squirrels had run ahead

for him and white owls
had turned and swooped
their heads as he passed
so he learned quickly,
despite malignance
that lay off to the side,
how to forge
and how to lead.

I cannot tell now
why I wanted to follow,
if it was an inborn wish
no longer to be frightened,
or taken on a dare
when nobody was looking,
only that the light
seemed endearing,
but now along
this strange path
that veers dangerously,
and even at times
with a graced sense
of the wildly improbable,
and always with a slight
and continuing rise,
it is everything.

The Basement

A sword left from the Civil War
hangs on a hook in the basement

and I remember wondering as a child
if it had done its duty: did it leave

bones behind; did it, from use, need
sharpening every week or so? It

invaded my dreams so I'd be its wielder,
its cleaner, its safe companion and bedmate;

the red tassel it sported is centuries' thin,
a lusterless flag now that bugles no longer

warn the forest air. It hangs next
to a hammer, on one side, and on the other

a chamois cloth for cleaning our car.
On the shelf above is an old Victrola

that used to sing pretty well, and farther on
a stiff catcher's mitt and a broken crucifix,

but, no doubt, the sword holds pride of place.

Law

for Ed Panelli

Sun, moon, planets
all have their pattern,
how redwoods grow
how hens give us
their fruit, how
our blood runs
in circles – this is a law
we know, it gives us
a base so we thrive;
scriptures, documents,
handshakes provide
the patterned words
for direction so we discern
the right; but thistles
spring up, words
are dissected, stretched,
and shaved, other words
creep in to question
and we are left floundering
in a world where shifts
in fault lines
create chaos,
where patterns have other
beginnings, so the robe
we've worn for safety
and grace is torn,

sidewalks and towers
and – children – are rent
in agony; we've learned
that law is not one
but many.

A mouse has one
an owl another.

Acorns

Every day is an acorn:
they pile up, bushel baskets
of them, get dried out

and crumble, but every once
in a while one grabs hold
of the earth and eats its life

and green seeps in,
runs through hours
and even years;

thus, at the end, all
the trouble of raking
and hauling was worth it.

My Cat

My cat does not like clouds;
she once tried to grab one

but it nestled around her,
ruffled her fur and sat

on her tongue so she's wary
of being out in the open

where toys can take control.

Burden

I know my ABC's, I can read a map
and even use an old car's clutch;

I've been known to give a lecture
or two, so don't stand there, one-eyed,
arms akimbo and imply it's time.

You haven't the beans to read me
and judge I'm ready;
your little mind
just wants a clean room with all circles
and rectangles in the right place
irrespective of their lilt
or the fun they have
in trying different patterns;

you see a Z where I see an A,
and my eyes have been sharpened for years
despite their use,
yours have been stuck
in a cellar with iPads for company.

Granted, it may be harder now to cut
my toenails and my eyebrows need
constant care

but because you're nimble
and well-groomed does not give you
the ticket to walk in and declare an end.

That burden is mine to declare.

So - go play.

The Shoveler

He started out early just as the sun
was winking its arrival, and he nodded,
"This is the day." So he marched to the spot,
measured four heartbeats long
and two wide and shoveled the first
clump of rich loam, laid it aside
for later, and then the second. He knew
his planting would take time, but he wanted
to do it carefully, as you'd sculpt a chunk
of marble to make it curve into grace,
because he's always honored the smallest
gesture, believing that we are given only
a certain number of them and that each one,
set beside the others, must mirror their beauty
and create the effect we leave behind.
He dug in again, watching the smaller
clumps slide down over the tip
of the shovel and back into the hole, then
a small root tugged at his shovel,
but he was patient and understood all the reluctance.
At noon, he brushed his pants and snapped
his gloves against the oak handle
then went in to rest before the long afternoon
when he'd have to measure more finely
because she was always concerned about how her clothes
fit or how the furniture was placed

and he wanted to arrange it all before the sun
left him and he'd then have to walk each
room, light the lamps and ensure
there were no more surprises, no more
ungainly gestures to put right.

My Dog, In Monterey

Do you remember, Pal,
walking along the beach
just at that moment
when the sand lit up
as the sun sank,

the horizon a line
of green and blue
and the leaning cypress,
tired of the wind,
turned grey?

That moment
when you jumped
for the stick the hundredth
time and never considered
it wasn't the first, that time

when time could not
be prolonged, no matter
how many prayers
were offered? There were
other days, packed

away in a special box
in the closet under the stairs

where only family ghosts,
hungry for nostalgia,
could rummage through them

to find both regret
and young pleasure.
But this day?
At its close, I put
a special ribbon on it

and placed it next to the clock
on my bedside table
where it remains still
so each morning can begin
with the light that bloomed that day.

Discernment

There's a piece of chocolate sitting smugly
on my desk and I'm looking at it carefully

wondering if a resolution taken in sanity
can overcome physical desire – and I know

that contest is a paradigm for my life so this
moment is another test; but let's pause,

re-consider and not invest too much
in one piece of chocolate, for it is a fairly

benign item: dark covering
with a vanilla cream center, laced

with a touch of orange essence, topped
with milk chocolate sprinkles and hiding

a thin layer of caramel as insulation.
But I am not interested, my former decision

is a strong one, it has helped me rise
in the morning, pay scant attention

to inferior rumblings and allowed me to conduct
a breakfast symphony with flaxseed, prunes

and plain toast. Then I wonder, sometimes,
if the hereafter will menu me the same, so I turn

to the chocolate sitting smugly on my desk
and with contrition accept its beguiling invitation.

Igdrasil

for Mike and Mary Ellen Fox

We owe much to trees:

redwood, oak and elm
cedar, banyan and cypress
straight, gnarled or bent
they teach us majesty;

in a world of fragile desires
we need enduring exemplars
to lean against.

They do not prevent
our arguments when blood
is spilled, they cannot smother
words or even graph
our loves, they cannot sift
our anger into smooth compassion
or bury our sorrows.

But with sacramental pride
they nurture in their arms
the smallest wings
of life

and bear an April beauty
through years of frost.

Like Igdrasil of old
they stretch out of mud
to haul down heaven
so one becomes the other.

They are still.

They grow without fear.

Nunc Dimittis

for those who knew Jerry McKevitt, S.J.

You lie now in your "Nunc Dimittis"
on a white sheet in a room
so white our eyes glaze;
we have shielded you before,
but now we can only stand
and offer an "Amen." Tinder
is fragile in a firestorm, and we all
know it is too late for protest.

Too late for the white slopes
of the Sierra, *pasta alla Romana*,
the King's bells that tolled
a daily obeisance among palms,
much too late for pastels,
for tarragon, salmon and pears,
and all your precise words
that humbly chart our story.

The charts they now read
are only flesh and cannot graph
the rainbow of pain, they do not know
the scarlet line that frightens
the bone. Can they tell: this blood,
will its rage turn tender?
Will it glow as on a black day
when the rim of the world blazes?

Soft, let the breezes blow
soft. Love and prayers
are what is left onstage: this hourly
watch is only backdrop.
But O Lord, such a play
it has been - bless it! Bless
its high design; when it burns,
the dawn will be a brighter flame.

Daily Exercise

Searching
for words:

hauling
long-forgotten

treasures
down

from a dusty
attic.

My Webster

I find this dictionary so hard to lift:
it's filled with the literature of the ages,

the correspondence of millennia, the recipes
of all gustatorial delights, and the bland

instructions for every gadget we've surrounded
ourselves with. It is a compendium of history

and a theological insight into the business
of God. There it sits on my bookshelf,

intimidating, quiet, deeply proud
of itself. But I tell you, my smug Webster,

that this morning's prayer could not find
the words it struggled for and though I paged

carefully and even tried a magnifying glass
I could give neither the pain of absence

nor the joy of presence a proper language.
Can it be my magnifying glass is not strong

enough, or are there words hidden behind
words? Have we yet to discover a vocabulary

trying to inch its way out of the chrysalis
of desire?

Faith

for Joe and Cathy DeMaria

It's a gift, you see,
the ability to look
at the branch of a tree
and note the life

inside, or feel
a rock and know
its hum is real,
to hear the words

of a song as it lifts
your heart and be grateful
that we are able to sift
matter into fine

juice; we are blessed
to hold a slice
of bread and rest
in the life inside.

The Play's Last Act

He's hiding somewhere, I know,
behind the sofa there or maybe
in the dark pocket of the closet;

I've searched everywhere, morning
and night, even under
the pink camellia bushes;

at sunset his black cloak
twitches the shadows, at sunrise
he hides behind riven leaves.

I've untangled bones in the attic
and unraveled old poems,
listened to foolish sybils;

if I could spy just his hem,
I'd snatch and hold and tie
him down and force an answer

but he'd be gone like mist in the sun:
he doesn't want to be found,
it's his game and his choice.

Mischief

He was riveting: his white beard
was a mop of magnificence, a symbol

of his stature as a man of means who stood
proud as an angel with an award-winning halo;

because of it, he could rise above a crowd
and ignore the gaze invariably fixed

upon it. He accompanied it into restaurants
where he adroitly avoided spillage

(onlookers took bets on his success)
and wandered through parks where birds

often attempted, with jealousy, to pluck
a hair for their adornment; barbers

never touched it because he felt sacramentals
should not be cheapened, and when he entered

the opera house, its tuba section
blared its applause. One day,

a small child jumped on his knee
and perhaps anxious for mischief thrust

her fingers into the white forest
but found only warmth and dappled

sunlight; ever after she enjoyed the company
of bearded gentlemen, and he learned

that docility in the face of rudeness
can spark a glow in a mischievous heart.

Harmony

for Jerry Alexanderson

Pay no attention to the sagging walls
in this room, they've grown tired of the noise
erupting from the ark at mealtimes, but it's unique,
isn't it?   A miniature version of the original,
I'm told. (Though historians are still divided:

some revel in fact, some
are content with an elusive note of poetry.)
But if you forget such details and admire
the architectural innovation and hallowed sweep
of the whole, you'll be transported into another age

where animals hugged and kissed like adolescents,
where such harmony has become a lost art –
not lost in Eden, but after the ark:
when Noah whistled them all on board
they leaped and scrambled in from fields

and caves, hearkening, too, to another,
stranger, voice that enveloped them like sunlight;
they marched in order, and quietly (though not without
exchanging whispered glances) and seemed
resigned to sit around for several months,

staring at stars that blinked in the rain,
listening to the wind that had burst from the fist

of the Lord and wondering if the grasses and fruits
that had grown so easily on their land
were to be replaced by shrunken husks and sand,

if the roaring over the white waters would kill
the music of their forests; they did not share
Noah's terrible faith, they lived
by what they saw and heard, so perhaps they cringed
in the stormy nights and bellowed their pain.

But Noah petted their necks and rubbed their
bellies, so they were comforted, they could feel his warmth
and heard the strength in his voice: for though his hands
could carve cedar, he softly caressed
his yellow-feathered finch; in the mornings,

he sang with the warbling bluebirds because in the midst
of thunder he had been allowed the grace of harmony
which eased open God's harrowing day for him
and dampened the fires of fear he felt
running along the sides of his old bones.

Now, if you look closely, you can see
each pair, male and female,
though you might miss the busy fleas
for they jump from place to place and were probably
the only species to have had regular dinners.

All in all, Noah kept
a tight ship and they are displayed here
as he had arranged them – a bountiful mix of color
and form, eager to dismount and begin
a new world of Darwinian persuasion.

Grandfather

"Then he will strip his sleeve and show his scars"
(Henry V, Act 4, scene 3)

I listened to him speak and watched his eyes
and thought: there's dusk behind the words,
not easily heard; he lifted his cane then thought
better of it, so settled back on the bench and watched
arrogant crows fill the oak tree; his head
moved like a robot, programmed from somewhere
hidden; mallard ducks on the pond swam
in a green daze and a yellow crocus
nestled near his foot. This was the time
he waited for each day, standing
in his open door for my arrival and if
I was late, he'd swing his cane like a latter-day
Charlie Chaplin, belying the seriousness
of his demeanor, for in all things he chose
the harder part, wrestling through life
as if a contest had to be won then tossed aside
because it never mattered. His shoes that morning,
and cuffs, too, were dusty as if the earth
was creeping up on him, taking as much
advantage as it could. I spoke little,
he preferred monologues and I gave him the space
he needed; his long sentences blipped
and paused and started over again with determination,

reflecting his gait, so I struggled to match
his rhythm and learned in the process how to grace
the battles that framed my own days.

Days in the Life

for Jeanine Conner

A slice of wanton wind
trembles one leaf
of a small bush set against
a wall; the other leaves,
still, watch the trembling
and wait their turn.

California poppies all
squinched up in the quiet morning
like arrows waiting for a target
but the eager sun spreads their orange
beauty across the field and they're assured
they're in the right place at the right time.

A soft slant of sunshine
on a back porch, blue
eyes that never strayed,
a cat lapping milk,
a plate of pasta putanesca
that made everyone laugh.

An unbent, stretching redwood,
its branches peering down at us
with amusing patience: we are Lilliputians
wandering its space in the cool

of a fading sun, trying
to glean its take on mortality.

Those first steps Jeanine
took across the long carpet,
pushing aside the hands
that hovered like baby angels,
but she fell and began to cry
because she so wanted to be an adult.

Two twin fawns
craning their new necks
and suckling at their mother's breast
while she munches, looking at me
with only a mild concern:
a morning bright feast for all of us.

God hit the mark every time.

Washington Avenue Bridge, Minneapolis

I don't trust the early morning joggings
out onto the high bridge over the Mississippi,

the one Berryman jumped off to find
a touch of meaning; or maybe it was to renounce

meaning. He stood tall in that last poetry
reading, stretching his words out as far as they'd go

and there we were trying to reach into them
before they sprang back into his mouth, spent.

I don't trust the jogging there because the river
is a Merlin who can breed sparkles of doubt

in its harsh whispering, hiding the mystery
that snagged Berryman's beard and coaxed him

with music he loved to wrestle with; I was hoping
for a twelfth address to the Lord, but he may

have been delivering that, softly, as he fell.

Daily Task

for Michael Zampelli, S.J.

How does he do that?
Tap it just the right way

so a facet is cleared,
tap it again and soon

this many-sided marvel
blinds us: I'd like to vise

the day that way, early,
use the fine chisel

of prayer

and by nightfall gaze
on splendor, twirl it

by moonlight and watch
darkness cringe,

say goodbye to the spirits
afraid of the glare

and welcome the angels
who keep my wonder

polished.

Apple Pie

I'm trying to make this short
like a note that has a simple

greeting, no more, so I can save
the best words for when we meet

because a face-to-face demands
honesty, the eyes tell it, notes

can hide behind a shy reserve
and keep the urges silent;

if I see you, it's warm apple pie
and that can never be ignored.

The Blue Heron

Eddie liked to box; earning $5
a night in those hot smoky arenas,

no bigger than a baby's bedroom,
he used muscle power because he felt

that's all he had, at least they told him so.
Punching the air as he walked to the ring,

he begged for applause, drank it in
as an alcoholic downs his first drink

of the day, then leaned through the ropes
to begin one more argument

with a strong presentation, a feint and dip,
a pulling back, a melodramatic pause:

he knew he'd win again. But he'd rather
be in a boat, rolling quietly on a morning

lake, waiting for fish to be surprised
by his invitation, and watching a tall blue

heron turn its head to look at him.
He liked watching. It was his form of thought.

As he stood, crouched in the ring, he watched
the slender moves of his night's opponent,

then watched his own glove move
like an easy ripple and dart! as the fish

is caught. Then he watched the open, blank
eyes of the fish as it lay, stunned,

ready to be stuffed into his basket
with the feathers of his blue heron.

Sitting On a Bench By The River

The reeds rustle so much
now that I am old,

they start music and each tune,
soft in the evening light,
hurts; it's the reaching back,
not to live again,
but to remember,
the pulling out of the muscles
and blood and lungs
all the neat
painful pictures
filled at the time
with the foam of the young:

we romped, sin-free, we thought,
through orchards of apples and plums,
jumped over broken chairs
and chased every bluebird
that tried to land; as we fell
into a pile of hay our laughter
shook her windows, but she laughed
right along with us – and that
was our redemption, whatever else befell.
That evening with the moon
an arc of diamonds gave us a glimpse
into how we should grow.

A mirror I hold now
to look behind.

Why should those crystal events
cause hurt so deep down it has no name?

Why do I dip my head
to ignore
the intervening years
while trailing my fingers in that river of the past
as if it held the only life
I ever wanted?

Do The Dance

You should dance more:
        get up
off your warm couch, stretch
your legs, rattle your fingers

and let everyone know
there's a buzzing bee in your loins
and a lop-sided squint
        in your mind;

throw off the mask of a beleaguered
Jeremiah and take a tilt
at the moon. Years are not
        elastic;

they're brittle, they chafe,
        they mock
your stance and hold tight
each of the minutes you spend

yawning. So lift off, do
        the dance,
and package those minutes with bright
ribbons – a gift to treasure.

When, at the last, you are asked,
"How did it go?" you might bemoan
        the sweat
but you'll invite them to dance.

The Gopher

Does this poor wretch ever tire of digging?
Or does it, rather, fire his heart

and bring peace? When he retires at night,
does he tell his children tales about the roots

he's encountered, the boulders that hide behind
soft loam – and the angry giants

that walk above? Does he accompany his mate
through the day's tunnel and show her the twists

and turns he had to make, the upward lunge
once in a while to spill out debris?

Sifting through his day, does he wonder
if there is a goal to celebrate when reached?

He's nervous around eschatological questions
and prefers the means rather than the end

because the means, he has learned, are all he has;
so it's best, he concludes, that he sharpen his talents

and continue to dig.

Images

The images won't leave me
as I walk here in the shade:

a boat ride, an island, a wide
grin; a ground squirrel,

unafraid, jumping on my knee;
a warm evening with Scrabble

as the house creaks against
the wind – they all get jumbled

and they're all tight with a pressure
that stops my breathing

and the hard edge of all
is that time transposes

days and words, muffles
voices and misinterprets.

Memory does not find
the truth but only a yearning,

yet here, under strong elms,
it knocks like truth.

Both Sides

He walked the country lanes
each night, not grieving –
he gave that up long ago -

but remembering each corner
how weeds would start in spring
and turn crinkly in autumn

how a calf would suddenly arrive
and fences begin to sag;
he watched the sun's shadows

stretch across the fields and reach
for his feet, then he would turn
and review it all the other way

because he believed that to know
something truly you had to take
time to see both sides.

The Wasp

The wasp is lonely.
He wakes each dawn
but finds no one to fly
or bite with him.
He wonders if the sun
that rises will have a message
for him but he's learned
to expect no voice
so he does what he does
best: challenging
those he touches
to notice the lesser
forms of God's
prodigality.

What We See

for Denise Levertov

Wooly my eyes are
they dart and fall
so often miss the mark
but now and then
blue lightning
shows the place:
I see a child of the desert
with strings for arms
and a large balloon
lodged in his stomach
with eyes so blank
they cannot even doubt
the world they see.
I want to say,
"Let's trade eyes,
you'll see the green
that sways in a morning
breeze and the white
froth that sprinkles
an ocean wave,
you'll see wildflowers
leaping and a sun
more gentle as it warms
a waiting spring;

you'll see light
as it glances off a glacier;
you'll see my hand
reaching to hold you."
And I'll see the arid
days you've lain in,
the stiff hours
that stopped and were afraid
to move on, the minutes
that lay scattered;
I'll see the shadows
that moved across your face;
I'll see the grain
of wheat that died
but could not rise.
You will see what was intended
and I will see what we have done.

It Takes Time

The leaves outside my window
are rampant, turning from red

to green, slowly: at first they
blush at the new light, but then

are envious of the rose that bursts
at the top and brushes them aside;

it takes time for them to consent
to their role as lady-in-waiting.

Corners

It's the corner of things you should look at:
the corner of a Rembrandt where the embers

of a fireplace glow, the corner of a room
where books half-read are waiting to offer

their next installment, the corners of an altar
where tremulous hands have so often lain,

or here on a map where the corners are forgotten
and children wonder, or, yes, the corner

of my heart where I push things that should be
at the center - these corners tell us

where meaning resides.

The Elephant and The Little Boy

The elephant stopped,
looked at the little boy
in front of him and considered:

"Is he sad, I wonder,
or are they tears left
from the rain last night?"

The little boy thought,
"He should use my mother's
moisturizer."

Bad Dreams

I was reading this morning by firelight, here
in my sweet lone cabin by the lake,

when the words seemed to stand up
on the page – tired perhaps of their ease,

or bored with the sameness they offered,
rebelling to try something new –

and started to move around, freely,
disinterested even in grammar or logic;

they jumped and frolicked like new lambs
in a green heaven, oddly ignorant

of any order determined by the needs
of their guide. I slammed the book shut

to keep them in place – it would not do
to have them romping through my room

uncontrolled, unable to fit cleanly
into either my own imagination or their maker's,

unable to return to the story they were meant
to tell. I cared for them, surely, but on this morning

by the serene lake which had always defended
me from bad dreams, I was more afraid

I'd walk from my own place and start wandering.

Varia

I

Hands on my face, curled up inside
and outside, I'm lying on a waffle iron
and the top is about to come down
to spread me beveled throughout the pan,
frizzled and puffed, ready for someone's
indigestion.

II

"We are all a bit straitlaced," she said,
leaning carelessly on her husband's
polo stick, "but peanut butter
remains our favorite condiment."
"Should not a horse come galloping
over the hedgerows?" I asked. "No,"
she replied, "all of this is quite incidental
to the search for truth. Which, my dear,
given the weather, will take some time."

III

She felt bored
standing on the sand
looking at the white

boat bobbing
on the blue waves
but as the silvered moon
rose on the horizon
she dropped pretensions
and stepped in, boldly,
to jumpstart
her life - again.

IV

He and she were a twosome
snuggling always in public
and even in private, at times,
but princesses and bullfrogs
weren't accepted in the polo set,
certainly not at table with white wine
and frog legs on the menu.
They whispered under the stars
their doleful tale, searched
sand dunes for a magic wand,
but remained stuck inside
their skin; all of heaven's cries
could not disrobe them
and all of hell's laments
could not end their love.

V

I sit content, watching the Alexanders and Hamlets
of my age cavort across the screen: I avoid
the rules, waiting for the word, searching for a touch,
listening for the one last song that will not die.

The Party

This tight hunting party
shooting quail that flap and dodge
unsuccessfully: I had too many
words, one or two were bound
to hit the mark. Green woods
shifting, leaves etched in silver;
I loved that time: a blessing made it
right before we marched out, wind
was salt on my tongue, moss covered
secrets we all knew. It happened,
in the morning, in weeds up to my thighs
that two children I saw high
on a cliff were fighting like crows,
snapping and then falling hitting
the dark rocks below: more
casualties of the day, bleaker rang
the bells for lunch. I remember a hand,
sprayed with red; I prayed words
that mumbled, could not catch flight.
They were strangers to our valley, orphans
without titles to tell us why.
The party went about its business
shooting and hitting, with words angrier
than usual, but a crop of quail ended up
dressed in finery on a long table

where we then all chattered endlessly
about the right technique in taking aim
and the way wind and words can sway
what we have so faithfully practiced.

On Reading Chaucer

for Louis St. Marie, S.J.

I saw a mouse
reading under a lamp
one day
and he seemed absorbed
in the amorous exploits
of the Wife of Bath;
I thought the Wife
had she known
would have been pleased
by the interest shown her
in the twenty-first century.

The Wind

"You see," she said, "things
run away from me: leaves, squirrels,
little girls, even the wind:
they blow past me, never turn
to look or to sigh. I wave at them,
but I do not like goodbyes. So,
I sit here now, with feet
rubbing the soft green grass
and wait for a hymn to soothe my limbs."
She rocked. I was new to the neighborhood,
could not always grasp the words
she used to weave her story; she seemed
to watch the world from the distance of a star
and her hands glided toward me like a spoon
in thick cream. "I was unkind once,
but that's over." Her eyes were not locked
into the past - they saw too clearly
the road dropping over the horizon -
but she spoke as if her words could parse her life
differently and result in a simpler sentence.
I jotted notes, sketched her brow,
asked if death was near. "Yes,
but life is nearer." She picked up the flyswatter
and I closed my pad and walked past her
out to the road where the wind blew strong.

A Star Broke Loose

for Margot Fonteyn, 1919-1991

Toes, gnarled, have tipped
and opened spirit

rubbed the stage floor dust
and lifted to their unique dreams
all those who stare in wonder;

how a step can sculpt eternity

how a hand can change dimensions

or how a cross-tied pointe
can untie flesh from earth.

In one balance, all movement stilled
and from there the circling began
as if a star broke loose
and shot on its own across the universe
to show a brighter path.

You brushed away the outside
stood on a dais of camellias
and built a place in magic:
no matter the last years

the enemy inside

you proved that attention to a turn
will mold your years in light.

"Master, I Want to See"

(Mark 10:51)

"Leopards and sunshine
falling through trees,
silently, lolling
on picnic tables,"
she says,
"and notice the leopard
lifting its paws -
how quaint!"
I'm tempted to question
her perception of reality
especially when peopled
with jungle creatures
but she insists there are moments
in our lives when
the ridiculous
will heal our souls
and lead us to see.

Price

Age does that, you know;
it creeps up and drives

a nail into your brain
so you're not sure what's

left or right or how you
lost the map, then you start

to read and can't find
the verb between subject

and object and napping
becomes so normal your open

eyes think they're wandering
in a dull fantasy land;

but all of that is nothing
to the dismay at what

you thought you'd find
in your hand but didn't.

No matter. Calling Mr. Jack,
Mr. Jill; a dryness that goes

to the soul - it's a price, but not
a bad one for allowing

us time to shift into a gear
we haven't yet used.

Goodbye

for Terry Mahan, S.J.

I've seen them shuffling down the hallways
bending over to scratch their shins then grab

the rail to right their balance; I've seen them
lying with mouth agape, their snore filling

the room and cracking any words I've tried
to say; I've seen them laughing with glee

when students arrive to sing or crying
when "Celeste Aida" fills their tiny rooms;

they are the ones I've known and held close,
they sowed the seeds of argument and love.

We do not know, at the start, how avenues
are blocked, where detours will lead us;

we walk together as if all the years ahead
were popcorn, beer and hot dogs on afternoon

Super Bowl weekends, a *"Gloria in excelsis"*
every day, the dime we find on a sidewalk a sign

that all shall be well. Then the sun begins to set
on an orange horizon; we prefer a story line

with added chapters but are content with the plot
as it has been written. Memory recalls a group portrait

where all wear knowing smiles: they are lovely,
their eyes sure, their arms spread wide and high.

Mountain Words

for Margaret Taylor

It had been a busy day, people hobbling
      crowds with bad breath
children though were a light
when they ran the world opened
      exploded
and laughter fell into everyone
he loved all, no doubt,
he ached to heal, to enfold
in the strength of a Samson
      but so needed
            a gap in time
                 to listen
here on this mountain where he learned
to know the echoes in the slight breeze
white rustlings
      of the night
he could feel life, as always,
be with his Father who knew
the strain, the pulling out of himself:
would there be, he asked, an end
he could relish
      would muscle hold?
and each morning his eyes
      brought flame

each morning his hands would lift
to touch age-old prayers
each morning his words flexed
       hard
as the stones of Golgotha.

Visitor

A horse splendidly white
walked into my office yesterday
he wanted to know if there were

job opportunities for a retired
fantasy figure; he was weary
of being on call in so many dreams

and I told him we were a small
family company that dealt
mainly in kitchen furniture

but he said he was used to kitchens
there was one widow who asked him
to dry her dishes every night

I tried to explain there is a difference
between a dream kitchen and a real
kitchen, that knives and fire

and falling pots can be hazardous
to a, well, a horse.
He seemed disappointed and drooped

his head; his flowing mane fell
to the ground and I reached to touch it -
it was, I found, real, after all.

Rose

for Gloria Citti

This little rose
is the best thing
I ever grew for you
on this small planet
you can take the dinosaurs
and mushrooms, the great
Himalayas, full of grandeur
(an indication of My size)
but this thing I hold:
a red petal of velvet,
an aroma that was mixed
long before you came,
the stately presence
that had lions roar
and butterflies flutter in delight -
that has my heart;
where did I get the idea?
I know that life is not simple
that beauty can be a task
that love can be traitorous
that the inches of life
you inhale day by day
seem never to end
and I know clouds can obliterate
the gardens you till

but trust me on this:
there is a moment
when the rose opens it secrets
and you will know.

St. Mary's Hospital, Room 237A

I walked out of the room
away from the whispering, from

eyes that cannot find a place;
how is it the world becomes

so small and so silent, stars
colliding would make but

a slight distraction, whiteness
hushes everything to a pinpoint.

We talked about papers,
I couldn't find a pen

so wandered for a bit, begging;
I had to go back for a moment

to remember, to touch again
what was gone, then finally sat

on the floor, against a long wall
hung with photographs of children

romping in a wide, blue field,
my soul chewing sand

because of all I did not do.

Verdict

They've put You on trial
I'm told:

it was whispered to me
proceedings are held tight
in a shuttered room
off the main corridor
bewhiskered senators
and flap-eared poets
sit on the jury
I'm told:

but I notice the sun
still shines
because at heart You're generous
and inclined to overlook petulance.

Friday's Rood

for Rob Scholla, S.J.

They have all departed
it is clearly the end

a little dust devil whirls
around two of the crosses
heavy still with weight

no one eager for the job
better to leave and hope
they can easily forget;

the middle cross stands empty
forlorn, aware
it had embraced for a time
a presence that welcomed
its arms, relied on its strength

now it leans crooked
ashamed of its duty

it could not know yet
its future as witness
as healer

so it waits to be used again

and in this it is prophetic.

Skipper

He was skipping along the edge
and could see the rocks below
but feared nothing as he skipped
because he was born in a tornado

and grew with wind, rain and noise
in his heart; he bellowed in class
and scared his teachers, swung
his arms with abandon and broke

vases, lamps and statues;
at night he battled his sheets and
always won; his dinner plate became
a maelstrom of colors and tastes.

So we did not watch carefully
as he skipped, trusting his familiarity
with disaster, and were surprised
he had a longing for peace.

Detour

There is another world out there,
on the other side of what we see
and you'd be surprised at the chaos -

lovely it is, where spiders are blue
diamonds, ants are instigators
of laughs and possums have lost

their shyness; there, we roam the land
greeting them as family, blessing
their naïve intrusion into our lives.

Here, we do not treat them well,
our fellow travelers, lower than us
on the chain of being, all the little

ones who spark the day; we
clothe them with fear or indifference,
unaware of a garden where all

were given names and invited
to the table, were handed tasks
which, bouncing with joy, they rushed

to fulfill; they, too, feasted on wine
and pomegranates and watched angels
hover; they lifted praise and found

the steps they had to take. Then a detour
was taken, but they didn't create the map,
they could only follow close behind.

The Prophet

He was a silly man, everyone knew it
and sometimes even he knew it

but usually he'd barge in and scatter
words around as if he were Midas

bestowing gold on grateful peasants
but he was unsure in firelight how

to interpret the words that grew
out of his soul and wondered how

he'd allowed a spirit to grab hold
when people only laughed at his ranting

even though he paraphrased Isaiah
and warned of the fissure in all our lives,

even though he stood strong in the sun
with arms beckoning and a voice honed

by the wind - though when alone
he wanted to tear his words apart

and let that wind carry them to another
fool so he'd be free to speak his own mind

but after all these years he wasn't sure
he'd be able to tell the difference.

On The Morning

She had often thought about Isaiah's banquet
of the Lord and wondered if there was a place
set for her; here, she ate her morning bread,

swept out the dust that filled
the corners of her room, then sitting in silence
she'd look into the clouds for the soft rain

that would fall on the hills and bring comfort;
she waited for a word that would lift the day
and envied the sparrows that knew their flight,

the long sweet grass that accepted
each season of birth and death,
the skipping lambs that never questioned;

an uneasiness gripped her in the tight evenings
and she woke often only to hear the click
of insects and the untroubled murmur of doves.

Then one day, beside the lake,
a word came to her and she turned to catch
all its inflections, gathering them in with hope,

storing them in a safe place where she could fondle
them at ease. Their memory accompanied her
and made her so bold that when he looked at her

she said, "Yes." The days after, she followed
and walked and listened; she served meals
and used her own words to guide

those in search of a shepherd, she led to him
the poor who opened their emptiness, she taught
a new prayer that asked for forgiveness.

Walking beside him often, she watched
how he touched a brow and made the whole
come to life, how a glance would change

a life. But it didn't last: she found herself
on a hill, catching his blood in her hands
and wondering if all she had invested was a dream.

On the morning, she sat in the garden and looked
ahead to the sweeping, the insects and doves
and knew that rain could bring no comfort.

A voice startled her, she turned but could not see;
then: "Mary." And everything lifted,
her place was set at last.

Query

You come by my room and I don't know
what to say: are you asking for directions
to the restaurant or are you searching
for the word that gives life? You are diffident,

unsure of your place and unwilling
to intrude, a small crocus in spring
trying to get at things first hand, and aware
there are larger blossoms, more intricate,

I might pay more attention to, but you always
have questions relevant to our common journey
so I ask you to specify, and much to my surprise
you kneel and ask how long the universe

will last; I reply it depends on your imagination:
can you foresee the extent to which our lives
are ordered: is there a clock in the universe
ticking the minutes - or a garden nurturing

something new so that time will have pity
and care for the newborn? Whether we
are at the end or the beginning is a question
we'll ponder over a glass of brandy.

Selected Poems from

THE RIGHT TAXI

Waiting

I awake, lie there, rise and sit on the edge of the bed,
wait for muscles to get the message, stand, move slowly,
step by inch - or: put my foot into a sock, it's tight,

my toenail spears a thread, take it off and try again -
or: spread the sheets, fluff the pillows, then wait
for cold water to turn hot for shaving, wait for coffee

to boil: that's just a few, but – oh – the time it takes,
the minutes spent on useless minutes, the lack
of an insistent motive, the wasted breaths Melville

could have easily filled; what hours can I count in a day
that tax the brain or fluff the heart? We squeeze them
in between and around the dallying, the waiting in offices

watching people waiting, in lines at the bank watching
people perplexed and bored, waiting; and what about
those waiting for the Parousia? Meanwhile canvases wait

for paint, paper waits for script, Twain waits to be read
and Hopper to be gazed upon, and loved. Perhaps that's it:
love has lost its force; otherwise, we'd pump the morning,

show Hopper to those who wait and invite everyone
to drop their socks and shaving cream for a golden ride
in a raft down a joyous Mississippi. Yes! we would.

The Loons

for Nelle Harper Lee

Rufus rode often
with his grandmother out onto the lake
where loons played and complained
through the night; though small, he plied
the oars well - he knew this
because her eyes told him so.
She recited from all the classics,
teaching him how to orate
with the rhythm of his arms: "O,"
she'd cry, "I have ta'en too little
care of this." And other words.
He stacked them up like waves
in his mind and they rolled in his dreams:
long sentences with ripples
in the middle, short phrases
that pounded his heart with her inflection
(stark, lonely, as if it were caught
surprised in a crater of the moon);
she washed words so they'd shine.
The loons followed her and when she spoke
they circled in silence.

Jeremiah On Wall Street

Bellowing and roaring
you march into my office
carrying your own private
brass band in your throat
to denounce the chaos
of our world and point
to so few rainbows and
how even they have grown
pale; I will sit stitched
and wait for the band
to wheeze itself out
then I will say that while
most in your circle would
look to Eden, I look to
Abraham for taking things
so seriously and to Moses
for disrupting well-organized
plans and to Jesus for being
such a stickler: discords,
all three of them;
they could not abide
the ancient harmony
flowing from mountaintops
the cloud-wrapped notes
that kept us free;
you it is who are chaos

smashing your way
through an order we have
sedulously resurrected;
so soften the decibels,
doff your scarf and move
to warmer climes.

Homecoming

You walked in lost, hair touched
by evening mist, light from candles
made you a rainbow - there you were
smiling so full of gladness

you had arrived but a little late
we were ready to hold you long, still
you stood dazed unable to believe
your journey over, the past healed

cries of dark winds pushed
away in caves buried in years
owls free now to dip
through the night, you watch them

and see the spirit of all you lost
but here now a press of love
I wanted to jump on your rainbow
and slide down with joy into your heart

to brush away the warped shadows
of ashen crossbeams to prove you were
right: mountains can be laid low
streams will jump and dance again.

Ebony Grace

She peers around the door, wary
of imposing: grey curly head
with ebony grace. She sees minutes
passing, too fast, reaches out
to halt them, punctuate her wish.
Time was, everyone marched
slowly under the hot sun and she
parsed with care for her charges:
a blackboard washed with chalk spelt
lessons too hard for some to learn,
but she pushed, and words began to grow,
pictures flamed; she knew where
to plant. Now, long past
those humid days wiped clean
with thin cotton, she limps in
and waits to be heard. Her eyes,
heavy with old light, ask
that the room pause, take note;
she cannot impart in a moment the violent
ignorance she has bloodied, the rage for those
who turned and stumbled into long ditches,
the loud joy she sang when a sharp,
tight bole broke into blossom.
She waits. As when a conductor
lifts his baton the silence builds,

the chattering now stops, strings
stretch unheard, waiting for the bow:
the hot sun shines through walls
of glass and she again begins to parse.

Father's Day

You turn with a question toward the whisper
the pine branch makes on the window
and then place before me a pad and pen
and say in case I need it there it is:

you do not say what course of thought
impels this offer. In your darkness
do you hope I'll write my soul
so you'll know what to say next

time I visit? It's hard for you to sit
and trade words; but that was always
true, you had looked at me and hoped
I'd hear what you couldn't say, then you'd

throw a punch in jest to teach me
what I refused to learn. These words
you want me to write now: would they translate
better than the silent ones before?

You had other sentences to arrange in your
tool shed, that fine prehistoric dictionary
whose puzzling alphabet only you understood;
but from those tools you fashioned our lives

and I thought God could not have done worse
if he had used the same for his own work.
I will entrust them now to archives
and pray for time to decipher them.

Cold footsteps in the hall remind us;
the pine branch is still. Perhaps
this is what keeps you here: waiting
for me to use the pad and pen.

Garden

She flounces in, carrying yet one
more vase, this one filled

with daffodils; a soldier, she arranges
her ammunition and secures unattended areas -

there's a dead spot right near
the bookcase, needs a bit of shoring up -

yellow should go well with the white roses
on the mantel and blue periwinkles on the coffee

table, which look across the room at calla
lilies standing proudly in an urn

near the door; there are violets and camellias,
baby's breath and, she thinks, what did I

miss? no, everything's set.
She has invited Nature to invade her salon

to combat the coughing that disrupts the silent
air; if the colors are properly mixed,

strewn about according to plan, then all
will be well; here and there a petal

falls, but they can be silently swept away; now, with curtains opened, sunshine can break in.

Encyclopedia

for the dynamic Novitiate class of 1951

I used to be afraid to touch
the ground here, the grass
crisp and alive, shadowed

by blocks of granite, but I wander
now, less like a visitor,
and note the smooth rusting

of names and dates; sounds
have grown softer, no empty
screeching, bluebells in the corner

give comfort. Yesterday,
the gardener mowed and lined
edges, making everyone

secure, their roofs neat
for colloquy; and in the sun I swing
my arms and stretch my legs

(the end of a run) and wonder
why we paint this scene
in crows and empty branches

for here, now, lies
an encyclopedia of love and hope,
a place to learn what others

suffer to know. The attempt
goes on outside the gates
but - the rest is here.

Roadrunner

"It's a bright and guilty world."
Michael O'Hara in "The Lady from Shanghai"

Only a child thinks forever:
having learned of no other possibilities
in the few years the three of them sat
hunched together for the evening news -
with a flip to the Roadrunner during commercials -
she presumed the conversation would continue;
she remembered, early on, the bustle
on oatmeal mornings, riding high
on her swing out by the long green beans,
and laughing as words made sense.
Sunshine was heavy then, burrowing
into the earth and exploding into sunflowers,
sweetpeas and blue larkspur - the blossoms
she'd pick and arrange around her day;
afterwards, she scattered the dried petals
as sacramental leavings of a finished task.
But she thought things human remained
(as she thought bones would always be straight):
then, without careful parsing, one went
one way, the other another,
and the evening news continued its digression;
mornings were quiet. She objected
she had not been prepared, that swings and beans

were no lesson, the sun should have hinted
at a colder language. You don't hear
whispers on a swing, she learned; you miss
eyes looking into the distance when the Roadrunner
has you riveted, wondering if once again
he'll evade doom. You don't notice
hands not touching and you don't know
about the black space when words fail.

Abundance

for Lorna Panelli

See this piece
of crystal
how the light
fractures?

It's the fracturing
of beauty
so there is more
to go around

to admire.
The earth opens
each day
that way

each time
a deer leaps
each time
you smile.

Decisions

I want to get the details down right:
she's standing, I'm told, on the edge
of a cliff, her sight skipping over
the massive ham-fisted rocks that

strut their way down toward Big Sur,
she's impressed, apparently, but still
wondering why the continent stops
here and not farther out, though happy

about the steep drop: she unties her
scarf and lets it blow billowing down
watching it catch at the air; they've
described her that way often and I'm

trying to get the colors right because
tone is important in a crisis, you want
to bring a soft brown in here and there
to balance the more aggressive reds

and greens, this one is going to be different,
it will speak of mystery - we're partial
to that - but there will be a homespun quality
to her stance, too, to take the edge off things.

Inquiry

for Bob Warren

I dusted
       carefully
fixed meticulously
my Windsor knot
noted eyes
       watching
and wondered, "Am
I in the right zoo?"

La Señora

The steps down were the most fearful, but she entered
the clanging train each morning, ankles full of water,

and tried to gulp down the day as if it were her last;
she pondered again the morning's words: "we shall all

be changed, changed utterly": hope dropped
into her hands: listening, Rodrigo's notes, bursting

from his darkness, sang in her heart: she was born
for Valencia, not this stinging dustbin of chewed gum

and urine, the left-overs of moles whose ride is a flight
into shadows. She wanted a royal mantilla and a sun

she'd gallop with down to the sea: bones to combat
chance, ankles to fit and arms bathed in cream;

then she'd lift her new voice in praise of the saints
and kneel at the high bell: cloisters would arch

her beauty; the sky would open and soft dust swirl
around her feet to glint the day. The train slowed

as she lifted her packages and walked out again
where she could not run and searched the passage

for a herald she prayed was there but could not hear.

Discreet

He sits with soup and a British thriller
alone, in a quiet St. Ives hotel

and while Mrs. Dawson is being butchered
he cannot help but hear another operation

whispered, and sees a hand brushed aside
but he turns it off, back to fiction

easier to concentrate on logic written
than illogic spoken; he follows the scent

then catches the steak beurre blanc
arriving at their table and they pause politely

he turns the page quickly, is this true?
They toast with red wine, she slams, sloshes

it on the table, hisses words never meant
and he's following his own words

mysteries have a puzzle of emotion often
difficult to grasp but he's content to know

solutions, now they rise and his hand moves
so slightly, the noise wakens them all

and when she falls he wishes he had not registered
in a "smart, stylish, and discreet hotel

near the water, known for its tranquility,"
because he's lost the line that separated

his table from theirs.

The Peg

for John Ottoboni

Each morning after a breakfast walk
I hang my sweater on a peg in the closet,

knowing it will be safe until I need
it again, because the peg is rooted

in a hidden beam that stretches from the cellar
to the roof, a sturdy tree that will hold

branches of other beams, plaster boards
and leaf-green wallpaper, portraits

of the past - and my favorite peg: I need
such strength for my peg, it must

be available for the worries I entrust to it before bed
and humble enough to bear cast-offs.

It's the one sure thing for the day,
like another's shot of brandy or someone

else's morning prayer; we depend
on such gear for their connection to the beam.

"La Bohème"

They're singing to beat the band
"La Bohème" coming out all
beef and whipped cream:

bravado, poverty and wine
but soft - hear how its melodies
dip, chasing a violin;

they rush to close the veins
of the soul, belie the Aristotelian
calm; if Mimi can so enter

and disrupt with her final plea
where can peace be found?
Her notes sting as I walk

to class; how shall I lie
about the knife at my throat?
It is terror we learn from love.

The Cat Starts Scratching

Young, the desire is not there:
no evil intent, or even
rudeness; the heart is not baked enough
to want the final touch; the brain
has no antecedents to know the lack.
What seemed piety, for most of us,
was either a need to please or a halting
attempt to discipline grace. Like
disciplining a cat. If peer
followed peer into the darkness and named
it light, there was, at least, company
and therefore corroboration. But two eggs
every morning, for years, you want
more. Some parts die
and they tug, not forgotten; some
start pulsing, urging, unready.
And the cats starts scratching; the light
is still darkness but it beckons, insistent,
then you know and desire finds its way.

Aunt Christine

While this is not what I would have chosen
I'll eat it anyway: Aunt Christine says we are a race
with few choices: hummingbirds and spiders
are a given, the sun rises and sets; the young
speed their years and the old lie waiting;

so anything presented on a plate by creation
is worthy of attention.   On another planet,
I would concur, but my slippery mind,
also presented to me without my request,
prefers to discern different steps

on the ladder of creation, to judge that blooming
roses are more aromatic than their roots,
that imagination can travel faster than snails,
Caravaggio's lines have more depth
than my stick drawings – that my soul hungers

in a way my toe cannot feel. Aunt Christine
gets lost easily: I have strengthened the fence
she has built around her life, the small acre
she knows so well: years earlier, someone
opened the gate for her; she slipped and fell

along the hillside; now she cooks my meals
brushes her skirts and sticks to the wisdom
of her enclosure. I am not ungrateful, so
I lean over and fork with regret the turnips
I wish, in her acre of content, she'd stop planting.

The Day

You said you wanted to die on a bright day
so you could find your way clearly to the shore;
you said noon would have no distracting shadows
to maneuver around, for you believed the lore

that the soul is haunted by them; you said the day
should be long because you never could walk fast
and you wanted not to be late; but here you are,
stretched out in dark winter, betrayed, long past

the summer's light; but is there ever, finally, a day
perfect for what you now know? Does our world
prepare us correctly, with its colors and its din,
for the moment we all shun when we are hurled

into silence? You do not speak. No matter the day,
then, no matter the silver clouds from the west:
you've packed away your trinkets and lie with empty
hands, ready for what someone else knows is best.

Belief

When I was young enough to believe,
we would wander through the old lot that snuggled up
against our house on the left; on the right
stood our orchard of apple and cherry trees,
an Eden of possibilities for the naive and hungry,
but on the left was mystery and, perhaps, revelation;
three great maples shaded
a timely riot of small discoveries:
blackberry bushes rooted and tangled
underneath lilacs, and under blackberries
grew wild strawberries, while up through
strawberries sprouted, each year,
early crocuses with their Easter colors
that initiated the summer canvas; soon,
here and there, in breathless clumps,
white lilies of the valley dropped
their sweet fragrance and thereby fastened
memory to a time and place. Bluebells
began, then wild roses
sprang out of vines and blushed as they climbed
the maples. Out of holes hidden
from long before our parents arrived
to claim the land, crawled mice,
gophers and green garters (but much
down there remained hidden).
We spent truant hours watching
this work, heeding woodpeckers and crickets,

sampling the fruit that ripened around us.
We did not understand attribution,
but the brushwork was impeccable; even the sky,
pale hot blue or exploding
with dark thunder, functioned as a backdrop
for the riot, and for those so young.
In such a way did the world fashion
our home and make it strong dogma.

Time Out

They noticed that the sun, in setting,
wedged itself between two sentinel trees
and couldn't budge. Since they
were not ready, they smiled at the opportunity
and moved down the street,
scuffing golden leaves, to say goodbye.
Long shadows bent around white walls
and painted a '52 Ford resting on
carefully arranged piles of brick;
a laugh broke through a bedroom window.
Red bougainvillea blossoms
tumbled across the pavement
promising a more lush return,
while Mrs. McLaughlin's water sprinkler worked
overtime on two corner rose bushes.
Danny and Joe wrestled on the front lawn,
ignoring pleas of "Bedtime."
"Not yet. Not dark yet."
Further along the street, they turned:
the voices were winding down
(but more slowly - even the streetlights,
following the City Council's schedule,
were clearly confused by the stranger light).
This was important: grass that needed cutting;
a fire hydrant that needed paint;
Mr. Larcher's front porch that needed support.
Was it the need that made them last?
And, then, the sun slipped through.

Marmathyn the Whale

Marmathyn the whale was content to flip his tail
and send spouts of water to the sun in delight,

he sounded well and full, then rushed up again
and burst into an air of wide horizons, free to laugh,

to wonder about the line where sea knits the sky
or how the wind, like him, can somersault the world;

and when great gales came he'd thrash the waves
to show them who's boss; though he hardly ever prayed.

One night a black deluge flipped him (he thought
of his birth and of how bright the sea then was,

how sparkles in a great blue tickled him, and he wished
he was there again when music seemed endless

and the smile that nuzzled him blessed him) -
and as he opened his mouth to cry for help

a clump of kelp plummeted in and ran along inside.
And then he prayed. He prayed

for three days in pain, looking for his sparkles in the blue,
begging the whale-god for a return to birth

so he could swim another way. In the quiet lingering
west of light he coughed, blinked, and took off

for a quieter sea; each night he'd pause in thanksgiving
but would never know he had saved a king and a city

and a simple man who had himself been in the throes of birth.

The Baseball Ticket

for Archie Simone

He was the one-eyed giant when we were young
handing out baseball tickets because he thought

that's what made us strong and I, burrowed into
Dickens, could not understand his predilection but

his kindness overrode any gravel I felt in my mind
and I clapped my hands, a twelve-year-old tyro,

so he'd know I loved him and understood his wish
to give us happiness; his last baseball ticket I found

in my desk and so though I didn't see the game
I hold it close and remember his one eye winking.

He Waited

He lay in his grave and heard faint voices
from above, then clumps of dirt, he supposed,

on the cover of his coffin; he wanted
to say, careful there, it's expensive oak

(at least they told him it would be)
but he wondered mostly about the next

step and how he was to extricate himself
in order to take it; he preferred light

to darkness, he told the priest, so he
presumed they had arranged it for him.

He took dips in the valley during his life
but they were for recreational purposes,

nothing serious, nothing to concern God
(who had bigger fish to fry), so he relaxed,

took stock of a contented life, and waited.

Modern Warfare

A cockroach clicks
across my floor
sniffing for grease
I lie bulky
bedridden
defenseless but for a boot
wait! I cannot
accuse it of martial
invasion
its intentions are benign
its heart an empty
shell of dark
yet
any advance
on my person
must be countered
with appropriate
severity
nations protect
their beaches
kings hold
fast their jewels
cannot I therefore
save
my bacon?

The Squirrel

for Bill Fulco, S.J.

The squirrel sits on the back
of the chair, tail twitching,
attention is set and he's ready
            to go
then he jumps on the lawn
runs circles, spies
a mate and chases (branches
are avenues, not obstacles) -
            then stops
                        and listens
hops back to the chair
once more at attention:
he has a deeper purpose there
his soul squeezed tight puzzling,
frantic, with percussive waves
against a little squirrel mind
            the way gets lost,
acorns sex and frolicking
get the better of him;
if he would hold his head
            still
for a moment - but then
he wouldn't be a squirrel.

Sunt Lacrimae Rerum

You sit there in a corner
two inches from the TV
to pick up on the political
palaver, no eyesight,
ears barely hearing
the arguments, but I marvel
at your persistence
and anger, that something
outside of your brokenness
can capture your imagination
and make it jump over hills
make it boil

there were moments
when the wind off the lake
blew open doors
and cleaned the whole house
but you stood hard
and held the walls
then the moon would rise
silver would break
the dark corners
and the house would sleep

the gardens now are soft
your lilacs
gave off their last scent

how will we know
to care for you?

The Egret

An egret stepped warily into the trattoria
on the corner and ordered a pasta with marinara;
the clientele paused as one pauses
when cocktail chatter is broken by a belch
or as happened the previous evening when a rhinoceros
waddled in for a martini: it was getting increasingly
difficult to eat without the odd interruption.
The owner (a Neapolitan) was open-minded:
he believed meals have a spiritual flavor
relished by all of God's kingdom,
that a table is the communal center of creation.
But his diners refused to countenance feathers
and snorts, to extend their fellowship to those
considered less favored in the chain of being.
Rumors spread about his tasteless predilection.
He lost business. The egret, though,
a snowy delight in his dark day,
chattered on about marketing, new customers,
seasoned opportunities, a unique vision
in an expanding world of gustation.
The Neapolitan - who first saw light
at the edge of a vast uncornered sea -
stood in the night and watched
the still stars, so far away.
They stayed bright, no matter
the turning of the world. He nodded,
returned to his kitchen, brushed the cobwebs,
and told the egret to open all the doors.

Teresa's Sparrow

This morning a sparrow flew in
and stood on my balcony, hesitated,
stepped closer and peeped in
at my reading of St. Teresa;

head skewed and eyes
blinking, as if listening to other
voices, searching another prize,
he seemed properly nonchalant,

but he noted - I think - with delight,
that Teresa floundered and fought
and prayed with startling sight
into the honor we owe to the God

who tackles us into life and shoves
us into prayer; stepping closer,
he dared the threshold, and since love
is the reason, I spread the page

for his perusal: what joy I noted
in his feathers as he pecked at the words:
but did he find a mystery coded
specially there for him

or was it a crumb I had dropped
from my morning snack? When finished,
he nodded winsomely and hopped
away. I was grateful for his attention.

The Right Taxi

for Jim Felt, S.J.

I

"Are you ready?" she asked. I was not ready
for her: black fingernails shone
off the bright screen and her spider smile
promised exactly what it could give. I sat there
in easy darkness with a silver beam
over my head, watching memory
locked in black and white images
that offered no conclusion. She smiled
invitingly, knew my heart's sore.

II

Outside, rain slanted
and taxis looked for home;
the day kept its grimness
in a tight fist and waited,
silently, for my exit.

III

We tend to look for poetry (I thought)
and wind up pasted on plastic
when what causes true pain
is the poetry in our hands - a primeval force

not remembered and not fought for
but sensed: no beam of light
pointing the way is needed: the elf
inside has learned his wisdom before.

IV

Before leaving, I watched animals
in two dimensions jump over rocks,
insects skitter around, ghosts
smile, saints find their place;
watched black lace and waltzes
(knew a quiet race in my blood).
Those flashing images helped me decode
a journey I had begun and wanted
to continue. So I walked out the door.

V

Poetry is like grace: it's there
without petition, but you still must ask,
you must ride the right taxi.
So I stood on the corner, with rain slanting
to see my face, and put out my hand.

Selected Poems from
THE ORPHAN BEAR

Le Morte D'arthur

In the middle of the lake,
an arm, clothed in white
samite, holds Excalibur.

When I was ten,
I wanted to ask,
"Didn't the white samite

get wet?" But
I was wise; you never
inquired about the obvious.

Or maybe I guessed –
pierced the teacher's
superior demeanor –

that Art and Reality
are two spinsters
having a feud.

At a simmering fifteen,
the sparkling white samite
moved in sinuous folds

and fell caressingly
on thighs that lay ready
in an imaginary tower.

At a post-graduate twenty-five,
and after Jessie Weston,
the mind clicked off,

in professional understatement,
each symbolic gesture,
each hyacinth girl:

the white samite
was key to the quest
and pointed to pale sorrow.

In England at thirty-five,
an adventurous skepticism
roamed Tintagel,

made the pilgrimage
to Glastonbury Tor
and squinted at the grave.

Finally, at my mellow end,
Mallory's dream
has entered my blood:

the white samite
tells my pain
and orders my world.

Paraphernalia

What do we get from all the connectedness
we've devised? My iPhone speaks to my iPad

which gurgles into my desktop and eventually
flashes onto my TV. What we do with wireless

we have done until now with sly looks, vocal chords,
flesh-on-flesh, even a kick in the butt; all of this,

however, has been digitalized to fit a more
convenient space; it's been diagrammatically

arranged for easier access, more effective control.
Circles have become squares, cloudbursts deleted,

I sit up straight rather than slouch, have forgotten
how to preface gracefully or conclude with a coda.

What do I get? I have become a shadow, a mite;
but if you threaten my paraphernalia, I can still bite.

White Swans

for Judy Dunbar

Pause now
and watch:

the sun's ready
to shine, to drop

sparkles, ignite
each house

with early dawn
with the song

of larks rising,
wait and see

if such a song
can burrow

into my heart
strip the old

shackles and reveal
a moment, clear

and just, pure
as the white swans

of Stratford, agile
as a wing aloft,

so I'm ready to greet
the day You've set

aside for me.

Why I'm Here

I'm waiting for this appointment, you see,
because last night as the stars looped
outside my window and beckoned me
to join their games, I felt intimidated
and knew I could not measure up – light
cannot find an entry into my heart –
so I turned aside to watch the wallpaper
grow.   That was boring and I realized
serious steps had to be taken; that's why
I'm here.   Well, this morning, too,
when the New York Times didn't arrive,
but on the doorstep I found only a squirrel
looking up at me with a smile of anticipation,
I figured there was more going on
than I could reasonably handle alone,
so here I am.   Oh, and my taxi ride here:
he insisted on driving past three
cemeteries because he divined I've built
a life on death, yes, I think it important
we lay orchids carefully on graves
to indicate beauty has been suspended
for a time, but that may not be why
I'm here; although when I was riding up
in the elevator, I could hear planets
move, and weeds were making a hell
of a noise (flowers don't make noise),
and though that happens rarely,

it may be worth a conversation or two.
When I walked in, your eyes were spinning –
they reminded me of the celestial rhythms
we were once so fond of – and when you said
I had to wait a bit, I was pleased because
I wanted to gather my ideas and render
them much more logical than perhaps
I've so far described them, but I tend to bare
all these experiences more candidly
than is proper so I apologize if I've embarrassed
you or taken advantage of your time:
your hands are so beautifully alive there,
held aloft over the computer keys as if
in amazement at what they are about to discover
but are waiting, too, for some surcease -
and the vision I now have of your place
in the universe may also be why I'm here.

A New Task

in memory of Gerard Manley Hopkins, S.J.

Do you, in your wild willful love, wander
through places you'd always longed for,

soft-step through forests of words
you glean like bursting mushrooms;

do you learn the trails and leave a leaf,
red with the rust of autumn, here and there,

to map your returns; have you discovered
the land your Greek verbs sang so sweetly of,

your Welsh nouns placed in woods and vales?
Do you see, finally, after the dimness

that shadowed your black-robed walks
down lanes of half-opened eyes,

all the sentences left to be completed?
Is your pen busy with new, full-blown

wonders - stanzas that startle the saints?
Startle them! Pleasure them with sound!

Even saints can learn a new language.

The Play

You come to an almost-end
and wonder if at any point
along the way you've hit
the mark, if the chalk lines
they've inscribed for you

have been followed; you
fear there were digressions
not planned for in rehearsal
and you may have even left
the stage for another play

or worked in the night
on a bare platform with no help
from your costars and ad-libbed
unnecessarily; but, after all,
some imagination had to come

into play, otherwise we squawk
like parrots and roam green
fields with no Falstaff as guide;
the aching question is whether
our imagination betrays us,

leads us to where home,
at last, will be lost,
or if it is a parallel web
of chalk lines meant to bolster
the original play.

The Orphan Bear

One evening as clouds of doubt pressed more boldly
than before, a bear with a bouquet of daffodils knocked

on my door. I thought: I should suspect door-ringing bears –
ought they not to be more blunt? But the bear's politeness

threw me off, and I agreed. He ponderously lay, an ancient
rug in front of my fireplace, and then slept, this orphan bear

whose rheumy eyes dreamed inward on a world of dark forests,
giant ferns and wide, pink streams. What would he turn into,

I wondered. This had to be a grim joke, this lump of primitive
muscle smiling silently in a living room in suburbia.

At the stroke of midnight, he stirred - but remained covered with fur.
He spoke softly then about the burdens of his mission,

his love for God, his troublesome back. I thought, why
confine myself to stray dogs - so I offered him my home,

my prayers, my own love. He nodded gratefully and placed
his great bear paw on my head. But, he said, he had a journey

to complete – and a touch of wizardry rumbled in his throat
as he sought to explain the years he'd yet to see. His wizardry

was comfort: he soothed the mourning fever that grew inside me
and eased the hollow wind that drops neither leaves nor rain,

for I had only painted clowns on bright walls; I needed his wisdom
to enchant, to dig further and etch a deeper vein.

But in the soft of night, he picked up his bouquet of daffodils,
bowed his head, and lumbered out the door.

Under the street lamp, he turned. "I will miss you," I called.
And I do.

Good Taste

for Don Dodson

I have a son, two years old, whose boldness is un-
rivaled: he has determined to take advantage of my
ample library. I would not object, in reasonable
circumstances, to his sampling each book, savor-
ing each poem, letting the words roll deliciously
over his tongue, for I've encouraged his literary
freedom and showed him delectable pictures, read
him stories of gourmet quality. In my world, children should be taught good taste.

But I walked in recently to peruse Hazlitt and
found my son eating him. My book lay in tatters.
Half the immortal words were digesting, mortally,
in the stomach of a boy who had learned to love the
classics. Since then, I have buried the Wife of Bath
and her fellow pilgrims, Othello, a white whale,
and a generous portion of Walt Whitman. Unable
to break his appetite, I have tried to encourage
a taste for Kingsley, Butler, and Beattie, but his
education has been too successful: he scorns the
appetizers and prefers strong meat. And in company, he amazes: he hiccups in iambic pentameters
and sneezes in couplets; he belches in breathtak-
ing stentorian indignation. At night, his dreams
rumble in an uncertain rhythm – with just a note
of classical cadence. (He has become, in so short a

time, a perspicacious critic of every word of mine: the lines he eats I mourn for; the lines he leaves I sweep away with yesterday's dust.)

What does one do with a son who devours libraries: hire him out as an editor? (The publishing world would thrive for he'd eat the gold and leave the dross for profit.) Put him to teach? (He'd frighten students who are used to a more genteel literary criticism.)

But sometimes, now, I notice he walks into the library with sadness – is it the tragedy in his bowels, or his own ingested perception that perfection of line has never been achieved and that his hunger will forever haunt him?

My second son will be educated in a sandbox.

History

for George Giacomini

When we think of the past, we have to be ruthless,
we have to jettison prejudices and dreams,

all the silver words we thought we heard,
all the dark strokes we may have painted;

that's what I do when I travel to the small space
back there in the tight box of my life

where larks seldom sang, but no ogres
rose from under the bridge, no nightmares

I could not combat; and if a werewolf moved
in the trees I could say it was not there.

I try to get close - knowing that lapses
are inevitable, the river switches course -

in order to see only a moment, hold it carefully,
whisk away the dust and hope it will shine.

If that can be done once, then a second time
is possible, and perhaps these stairs eventually

will form a ladder and I'll be able to climb
to a clean history, a portrait with the brush of truth.

The Kneelers

The old retainer, bent now,
dusts the top of the altar
every morning at nine,
kneels to brush the cobwebs,
then drinks what's left of the wine:
no one notices because prayer
captures all their attention.
They're searching the "wine of life,"
they say, and return to their knees.
He has knelt too many years
to expect spiritual enlightenment
on the floor, but doesn't begrudge them;
his knees were always less nimble.
At twelve he serves the stew
then adds a drop of claret,
for himself, to enliven the carrots;
from four to six he cleans
the living quarters, chasing mice
from under the beds and sweeping
away sweet memories,
while testing the Abbot's brandy;
at eight he kneels in the kitchen
to clean the lower cupboard
where the Sunday sauterne is kept,
then allows himself a joyous dance
in the garden's soft moonlight,

mimicking David before the Ark;
at nine he's back at the altar
preparing bread and wine
for the morning's ritual.
He's refused lighter positions,
insisting that kneeling is invigorating,
that the monks could not survive
without his solicitude for the details
and left-overs of life.
He's the quiet presence that makes
their isolation possible, and he is aware
that daily and adequate compensations
come in many ways.

Boston, April 15, 2013

I was intent on running and avoiding
the knock-kneed, grey-headed bumbler
in front of me who was only there
for a lark, breathless though he surely was;
his elbows, like sharp ravens, pecked at me;
his sweat, flung back, stung my eyes.

We were all in the same churning wave
rolling down Boylston Street, for fun, for fame,
for a camera's eye, for showing off the stripped-down
vehicle we had molded for the pleasure of molding,
for the challenge of the finish line and to drink in
the applause that showered us like cool water;

but the grey-headed bumbler was scissoring me,
his legs flailing, amateur muscles jumping
this way and that like a drunk daddy-long-legs;
hemmed in by tanks on either side, I hung back,
took a new breath and watched for the window,
determined I'd show him who was boss.

Then, my ears could not hear, a hard pillow
thumped me in the face and an army of needles
attacked my knees. We wonder, in a split second
sometimes, if what we have gained from life is finally
all loss, if running to keep in front leaves us, at last,
without legs, on a hot, red pavement.

Memory is a puzzle of a thousand pieces
we labor over to fit together the past, but the only piece
I now have in my hand is that of a grey-headed bumbler,
bent over me, his lips moving in words I could not hear,
squeezing my thighs to stop my life from leaving,
and I do not know his name.

What Were You Like, Really?

for Charley Phipps, S.J.

What were you like, really?
I know the plot, the parables,
the swine skipping off the cliff;
but in the morning, before the crowds,

when milk and bread were on the table
and the sun was just reaching,
when empty doorways spoke silence,
did you lean back and yawn?

Who wiped the table?
Were your sandals tight?
We watch you move and heal
and we know the power distilled in a tear,

we watch great clouds descend
in a transfiguring light
and all these we parse
with a 2000-year-old history;

but it's the cups and saucers
I want to know
because there your smile is revealed
as the day sets out

as the work begins.

Jumpers

Have you watched them? All the jumpers?
Rabbits, kangaroos, grasshoppers, all those

God has given a special talent of being light
on their feet?   They quietly share a secret:

an ability to touch a space others cannot reach,
and they know if they can hold that space,

encircle it, they won't begrudge their big feet.

The Maker

for Bruce Beasley

I can't sit here staring at a ceramic horse
all afternoon watching the sun move

from snout to rump and not think idly
that its maker must have adored his subject

so lovingly does it curve and swell, so
majestic its intent; how fondly has he

smoothed its neck and taught us tension,
how carefully the lesson expressed

that one must become something other
when one creates, something close

to an afternoon's movement of the sun.

Adam

That first moment I awoke
and my life stepped into time,

I let go the earlier years –
lying lifeless in a no-past -

and began to record
the movement of the sun

to translate my growing limbs;
strange to note how the death

of a rose could help me fit
time and place and how

the birth of a cub could give me
wonder; how great trees mocked

my new days; how marvelous
that she who stood beside me,

whose eyes slowly opened
on a green expanse that flowed

to an horizon we had not known
could so easily show me

how *love* begins.

The Old Chair

We never walked the same path,
though we tried a few walks together
one year, looking at the sky
and marveling at the distance in space;

we never paced the same room
though we inhabited the same house
and read the same papers on mornings
that never became distinct enough.

We never spoke. A wave across a lawn,
an attempt to explain my day
(a filial privilege compromised by haste) -
these glanced off, dribbled away,

like the words you tried to use
at the end. We never touched,
except in gentlemanly greeting. The wonder
of all is that you are nearer now,

in the back of my car, behind the music
I play, between the words on this page,
than ever you were when you sat, hunched,
in the old chair you loved at home.

The Barnyard

So bring them all in, gather the geese,
chickens, the donkey, make room for the cow

even the annoying rooster who hasn't
a good word for anyone, empty the barnyard,

we want all of you to be safe here where
the fire burns warm and we can enjoy

your company; it's not often a guest arrives
so sit quietly while we bathe his feet and mix

the corn; I've heard his glance can turn a head
and make granite blanch; I've heard his touch

can paralyze the underworld, his word can halt
lightning; but do not be intimidated, he wants

only a rest and welcomes your comments
because you, too, have a stake in this endeavor;

you, too, note human folly but have always
remained still: now, speak up and air your

wisdom, let him know he has friends who will
guard his walk, carry him along the lane,

crow when a traitorous word is spoken.
He is happy to receive any help you can give.

Fine Wine

He felt sometimes he was talking to wood
       to scarecrows
        hay-for-brains
he loved them but they could not imagine
his plight.
He spent dusty hours on roads of Galilee
words spilled out hour by hour
and they lapped it up thinking it milk
when it was fine wine they had never
        tasted.
At night when moonlight was hesitant
and the waves of Genesaret fell asleep
he'd walk the sand and hold the scent
of evening blossoms
        in his hand
and feel his Father close:
        that healed the wounds.
At daybreak he'd try again
he'd try again with a grain of wheat.

St. George

for Dana Gioia

If isn't often I'm invited to meet a visiting poet
so I accepted the invitation even though my soul

was chattering in anticipation and right to my fingertips
I felt a buzz because you can't approach Mt. Parnassus

without knowing you're just a shadow of trees on its flank;
you may strut like a dragon, puffing your blue smoke

in the dusty alleyways of a student's mind, but dragons
are notoriously made of paper and glue, not ready

for a St. George glaring down at the receiving line;
I bungled in and though I felt like I'd dropped my trousers

in the middle of "La Bohème" I greeted him and spoke
of his articulate mastery, his indelible line, his arching music,

not to mention his diaphanous allusions, but the twinkle
in his eyes then turned me honest: "Your poems bring me

joy." He took my arm and we strolled through a garden
of magnolia trees, azaleas and forget-me-nots,

fondling words and leaping over long sentences
until the party noise collapsed and dawn arose;

he thanked me, and as he walked away into the light,
I saw under his cloak the gleam of a silver scabbard.

Remembering El Salvador Jesuit Martyrs Of November 16, 1989

*"These martyrs were killed for the way they lived,
that is, for how they expressed their faith in love."
Dean Brackley, S.J.*

I am a garden
Yo soy un jardín
I grow the *Flor de Izote* and *Loroco*
and orchids that blush with morning's light
seeds are deep in me
       they die
and then burst into the colors I love

I am one with every world of spring

I glow in the sunlight
and dance in the breeze
I lie open to what my gardener desires

but seeds are different
and there are different desires:
that morning, early,
eight seeds fell into my soil

there were footsteps and clamoring
the breeze had stilled
so harsh sounds ricocheted
and my dust hung lifeless in the air
my autumn leaves shriveled

I felt the weight of impress
of possible new planting.

Now, I grow stronger
and bloom with a fresh grace
            each year
petals livelier than before
send their scent
out on an eager breeze

to tell the news:

Yo soy un jardín nuevo.

A Fitting

He's looking for a pair of pants,
simple enough, one that will fit

the growing contours of thighs, butt,
and embarrassing waist and it's undressing

and trying and fitting that's tedious
because cloth and contour seldom

match: like trying to fit
the soul into dogma, a laugh

into a new neighborhood
or a Hummer into a 1930's garage -

and how did Noah really fit
all those animals into his boat?

He kneels in the evening and prays
that he will fit into the Kingdom

where the sizes, he is reminded,
range from X Small Pygmy to XXX Large Tall -

that's some consolation.

My Uncle

My uncle woke early, shouldered a length
of rope and went out with Rover and Hi Ho to pull

tree trunks out of the ground: Rover barked
encouragement and Hi Ho had to pull, with my uncle

jostling and wrenching and getting his sockets yanked.
The sun inched upward and spread a golden glow

on the early mist: he tried to inhale what he felt
that cold morning, to keep it stored in his lungs

so it could spring out later when he needed it, when the pots
and pans took over; he had never expected to find

treasure on this land, his days wore on as he was told
they would; he had vowed to keep them clean, never

to barter them away and he was regarded as upright, a man
with pressed trousers when necessary and a well-shaven smile.

In the evening, after he scrubbed, he was rewarded with a beer
and newspaper, meat and potatoes. "Love is ever

a stretch," he'd tell me. His eyes had beamed when Hi Ho
brought forth a foal but of late they had darkened often,

even in the bright haying fall when the air felt
sharp. The promises he had made limped along

without foresight, scraggly, in need of brushing. "I need
to wash my lungs," he said, and when he walked the lane

at night he was waiting, I think, not for a dream
as you and I would but for another cold morning

to provide the test he needed for faith.

A Round Man

While I wait to enter the room
where they're all gathered, singing,

I think on why they're there and why
I've been invited: he was a round

man who could squeeze into any hole,
a malleable peg who disdained

dimensions and touted freedom
from rectangular certainty; he rolled

down a hill once to prove obstacles
were merely a distraction and if cuts

and bruises resulted, his rowdy
laugh would convert the most serious

of us and we'd all, for a time, hop
on the wagon; but a life commitment

to fluidity is treacherous: angles
form the contours of our lives

so we have to turn correctly if we're to move;
stop and go's help us maneuver.

Well, at the end, he had to be content
with a rectangular coffin, six

evenly-placed candles and me,
the presider, who now has to extol

in chiseled language and formulaic ritual
a spirit who could never be contained.

Perhaps inviting me for the office
was his last attempt to lure me in.

May angels lead him to Paradise.

Jolly Green Giant

for Marge Jonas

They came in all sizes – playfully jostling and cracking
   knuckles - from a bearded Lilliputian alcoholic

to a Jolly Green Giant of a woman who cheerfully
   wore a bikini; brandishing white banners,

and wearing smiles designed to melt clouds
   and make even the largest star collapse in a giggle,

they walked resolutely through the Pearly Gates
   and asked a feathered creature to see the Supervisor;

all conversation, hitherto delicately joyous, ceased.
   Eyes turned to this rag tag crowd, wondering

what creation had wrought: from what belly of what planet
   had come these intruders: had Love really fashioned

what stood before them all? Or had the universe reneged
   on its promise of an orderly evolution? They recalled

their own entrance when, to relieve their anxieties,
   soft music accompanied the opening of the gates

and ushered them from flesh to spirit, gently,
  distracting them from the noise of final rites.

But this crowd needed no distraction: they snapped
  their fingers, moved to a raucous rhythm (unblessed?)

and held out fleshly hands to clasp in companionship.
  What occurs in the smoke and mirrors of another dimension

is not readily observable, so we cannot say exactly
  how the two joined forces, laid plans for wider avenues,

and composed a new music, but the feathered creatures,
  it is rumored, stood agog as the Jolly Green Giant bumped

her way down the avenue, passed out scotch and sodas,
  and settled back for her daily conversation with the Supervisor.

The Walker

for Leo Hombach, S.J.

You offer me a walker, and I suppose
it's time: a necessary nonsense,

to be slighted but used as needed,
and I wonder what else we use

to maneuver; what rigs do we construct
to steer our way? Here I am often,

in the midst of prayer, and I cannot
find a crutch to lead me on to where

I want to go and I wonder if I am
mistaken, if the rig I want is not mine

to find, not mine to hold, but someone else's.

If I Should Die

If I should die before you,
would you make sure my sheets
are clean, my sink is washed

and my hair is combed in its usual
fashion; would you lower the radio's
volume (even Mozart shouldn't intrude),

and delete all messages on my laptop:
treat it as if it, too, has succumbed
to the inevitable and can no longer

receive and send; it will eventually
accept its destiny. Whisper
to my orchid, then bless it. Polish

my doorknobs: I want no fingerprints
left as a residue of my entrances
and exits; shine my shoes

to indicate I've always walked
on the bright side of the street;
and throw my umbrella away:

it was a good companion, but I'd not
want it protecting another's secrets.
Say a prayer, of course; even a mumble

would help; I've mumbled plenty
in my own life and have hoped
I'd be interpreted correctly,

but we don't know, do we?
Try it, anyway, and while you're
kneeling, in shadows and with candles,

recall, if you can, the moments of small
importance, the ones we dismissed -
they have left words that have lingered.

The Terrible Point

You never know
where you're going
when you pray:
buses honk
and pages turn,
people run in front
and trip intentions;
it takes time
to pause, reach
into silence, but
once there,
a train takes over
and the terrible point
is you can't direct
the driver, a wizard
who sits dark
behind a hard partition -
not like the movie,
with green smoke
(but with truer magic).
Along the way,
you stop, get out
and walk around the dancers,
watch the fireflies;
a trumpet sounds,
insistent, so you jump
and try the journey again.

No other traveler
for company, just a box
filled with notes and books,
carved animals and canes,
and still they take up
space you want
for other things,
for wondering how
you got aboard,
or how the train winds
its way without a map.

Transfiguration

I like the daffodils out there:
their long-stemmed insistence
on being first

I like at this time
the small green knobs
pushing against the earth

we know it happens
often, rain clouds
step aside
and bow to a day of light -
but surprise, always,
ice shifts into sun:

farther down than we can go
lies the straining bulb

not a thing to re-plant
but a Word to explode
break into colors
that leap through centuries
of gravel, of wrong turns
to be our yellow umbrellas

this breath that hallows

this gift that splits the old
worn rocks
and flowers in our prayer.

These Old Hands

I'm not sure how to begin this –
swallows darting in and around my brain
make my earth a little tipsy –
but I trust that one phrase will catapult me
onto the on-ramp and I'll be in the game.

I happened one day. . . .

and that's how we'll begin. . . .

to look at my hands and found lines
and markings I had not noticed before,

haphazard lines
indicating no one labor or goal

markings of old scars
telling me these hands had fended off
detractors, as if raw battles had been my life

so I searched old letters
newspaper clippings heavy with years
and full of sorry surprises
ran through photographs
(old smiles of old friends).

Not one could testify,
not one could fill in the puzzle,
not one could play the music which would unfold
my memory.

But I will care for them, these old hands
that know more than I do and so need
a daily blessing

these old hands that lift and grasp and caress
and point the way, unerringly. . . .

and that's how we'll end.

The day becomes more solemn and serene
When noon is past – there is a harmony
In autumn, and lustre in its sky,
Which through the summer is not heard or seen,
As if it could not be, as if it had not been!

Percy Bysshe Shelley
Hymn to Intellectual Beauty

ACKNOWLEDGMENTS

THE FOLLOWING POEMS, INCLUDED IN this volume, have been previously published; some of them have undergone slight alterations since their initial publication.

"Ebony Grace," *Negative Capability*
"Father's Day," *The Critic*
"Garden," *Interpreter's House, Oxford*
"Decisions," *Connecticut Review*
"La Señora," Copyright 2011 by The Johns Hopkins Press, first appearing in *Spiritus, A Journal of Christian Spirituality* 11.1 (2011). Reprinted with the permission of The Johns Hopkins Press.
"Modern Warfare" (March 26, 2007), "Abundance" (Feb. 28, 2011), "The Day" (Nov.7, 2011), have their original publication in *America* and are reprinted with the permission of America Press, Inc., americamagazine.org
"Roadrunner," *The Santa Clara Review* and *Studies in Jesuit Spirituality*
"The Maker," *The Santa Clara Review*
"The Cat Starts Scratching" and "The Walker," *Studies in Jesuit Spirituality*
"The Old Chair," *Jesuit Province of California Website*
"Time Out," *San Jose Studies*
"Belief," *Writer's Forum*
"Teresa's Sparrow" and "The Terrible Point," *The Penwood Review*
"Transfiguration," *Sacred Journey*

"The Orphan Bear" and "Good Taste," ***The Kansas Quarterly***
"Le Morte d'Arthur," ***The CEA Critic***
"Games" and "West Egg," ***University of Portland Review***
"Arachnoid Tempo," ***Pierian Spring***

Special thanks to my perceptive reader, James Torrens, S.J., and to Arthur Liebscher, S.J., for his generosity.